THE
DANCING
QUILL

"He died that I may live to tell my tale."

A. ANATO SWU

Published by
Maurice Wylie Media
143 Northumberland Street
BELFAST
Northern Ireland
BT13 2JF (UK)

Publishers' statement: Throughout this book the love for our God is such that whenever we refer to Him we honour with Capitals. On the other hand, when referring to the devil, we refuse to acknowledge him with any honour to the point of violating grammatical rule and withholding capitalisation.

For more information visit
www.MauriceWylieMedia.com

DEDICATED TO...

The Almighty God
and
'Mama Rose' Maureen Wylie

CONTENTS

ACKNOWLEDGEMENTS

Natural words at this point does not expound the way my heart is thankful for the saving power of my Lord and Saviour Jesus Christ. Like the centurion (Luke 7), I can say, I am not worthy for the Lord to enter this house of mine, called my spirit. But through the Master reaching down into me, I call Him Lord of this home. Thank you, Jesus!

I am convinced to the core that God heard my Mum's prayers and poured out His blessing of love, grace, health, wisdom and knowledge on me, that I may be able to carry out my given tasks without any hindrance. Dear Mum, may God continue to bless you and use you for His Kingdom, you have always been my inspiration at my side.

I cannot go another word without expressing to you the reader, that 'The Dancing Quill' is in your hand today because of the relentless efforts and sacrifice of God's own 'hand-picked couple' who always keep pushing me on and on through prayers, kind deeds, inspirational talks, and encouraging words. Thank you, "Mama" Maureen Wylie and "Papa" Maurice Wylie, for your immense love, support and belief in me. A good number of poems in this collection have been composed after drawing inspiration from conversations, pictures, songs, messages, and life experiences shared with love by "Mama" Maureen.

I am honoured and so indebted to Maurice Wylie Media (MWM) for taking up the responsibility of publishing my books. May Heaven's choicest blessings be poured upon its founder, Maurice Wylie, and every other individual working, or associated with the MWM.

I wish to thank Ms. Kuholy Chishi and my one and only sister, Ms. Aghali Swu for their support and encouragement in my venture as a fledging poet-writer.

For you the reader, may the fragrance of my Lord and Saviour rest on you, may you find Him within each poem and may you come to know Him in a greater way.

The Dancing Quill

A. Anato Swu

INTRODUCTION

I never knew that certain habits I inculcated during my dark season of abusing drugs would someday give me hope to live on and encourage me to build my future on it whilst breaking the shackles of addictions. As a budding science student with a unique record of repeated poor performances in English examinations, I disfavoured English language and hardly gave any interest to read, or write, or speak English fluently.

However, all this changed when I, most ironically, started abusing drugs while pursuing my career to become a top surgeon in one of the premier medical institutes, located far-away from my hometown...

Under the influence of drugs, I developed the interest to read English dailies and magazines, and would have read them every single day for hours late deep into the night. When I'd consume all the materials at my disposal then I would start reading my Bible, and though it served only as a substitute in the absence of any other book, or magazine or newspapers, I slowly developed a new interest in the stories contained particularly, in the Old Testament. Soon I'd have read the whole of the Bible, including the New Testament, but I'd remember only a few things. However, from those few things, I realised that there was someone (known to me now) as, the God of the New Beginnings, who had already died for my sins... my evil habits, and I could take these habits to Him, if I desired to be rid of them especially my drug and alcohol abuse.

When sense finally prevailed and I could overcome my addictions, I thought of sharing my story and that is how my first book 'A Diamond of Dust' was published as a token of gratitude to God for giving me a second chance to live 'In and With His Purpose'. Simultaneously, 'The Dancing Quill' that is in your hand today was made possible after I was made to realise that...

I am but the Dancing Quill
Who scripts according to the will
Of my God who gave me reasons
To survive all dark seasons.

And what I script today
Was taught to me yesterday,
As I read deep into the night
Und'r dark drugs delight.

The merciful, kind and loving nature of our Lord Jesus guided and shaped my thoughts, and enabled me to script what He placed in my heart and mind. He allowed me to draw out words, lines and rhymes from His bottomless well of wisdom and knowledge, after providing me with a particular theme.

On my own, it would have been quite beyond my limited education to compose even a single, meaningful poem. Along with His gift of 'A Second Chance' the Lord presented me with the Quill and gave me the privilege to explore life, love and nature. In all humility I thank the good Lord for saving my life and giving me a purpose to live, when the world had already given up on me as "A Hopeless Case".

At some point we all walk through, '... the valley of the shadow of death.' (Psalm 23:4) But we need to remember not to 'fear'. Why? Because "God is with me!"

As 'The Quill' takes you on the journey, know that God has a plan and purpose for your life too.

A Diamond of Dust

I sparkle in the light,
Like a diamond bright,
Reflecting hopeful rays,
In my own glorious ways!
With light I have no sorrow,
And bother not for tomorrow;
I'm not restricted to movement,
And I always shine in my moment.
I have no guarantee about t'e future;
T'e present is what I cherish and nurture.

I am a grain o' dust,
Living and dying fast.
I keep no oath or bond
To shine like a diamond;
I just let in the rays of light
To live my moment in delight!
I do not toil, or in doubt, ponder,
But allow t'e light to do its wonder.
And Lo! As I scintillate with the light,
I become a diamond o' dust to your sight!

Be a diamond o' dust!
T'e invite maybe thy last,
To forsake t'e worldly ways;
Hearken to w'at t'e Light says:
Leave t'e dark and forbidden place,
Bask in the rays and reflect His grace,
Open and allow t'e Light into thy heart,
Rejoice in t'is opportunity for a fresh start!
Tomorrow is not guaranteed, so shine today-
Live best thy life in t'e Light before ye go away!

My Beautiful Red Rose

(Dedicated to Mama Maureen Wylie)

Blooming rich and rare in God's own garden,
Like t'e first rose by the cool waters of Eden;
Behold her, dancing happy in t'e gentle wind,
My beautiful red rose of t'e most pretty kind.

Her fragrance angels love to wear,
Her bloom to sight so lovely dear,
Her stalk ever strong and unbending,
Her leaves evergreen, unwithering.

Care and tended by the sole Gardener;
Watered by Heaven's blessed shower;
Ever watched aft'r by love so personal,
My lovely Rose blooms for one and all.

Layers after layers of scarlet virgin petals,
She opens up for the pleasure of mortals.
Yet lesser does she desires of her bloom,
T'at greater be His glory over e'ery gloom.

Pollen from her age-graced ripen'd body
Spread forth as essence for ill's remedy;
Scatter'd by her butterfly to world distant,
Her memory we'll carry in mind constant.

Pluck her not but let her bloom undefiled.
Bloom of grace and charity quite unrivalled;
She lives in simulation of the greatest love
That we all be blest as desired from above.

My Supplication

Give me a place to dance.
So that I can romance
With the God of the second chance.

Give me a stage to act.
So that I can enact
My given role even though I'm imperfect.

Give me the ink for my Quill.
So that I can script His will
For humanity to learn how to remain still.

Give me a space to walk.
So that I can cross the miles and talk
With my God who holds me in times dark.

Give me the strength to fight.
So that I can battle with all my might
With my adversary and cast him out of my sight.

Give me my wings to fly.
So that I can try and try,
Until there be no more reasons to cry.

Give me a chance to speak
So that my tongue can be at its peak
To tell about His blessings to those who seek

Give me no more tears to shed.
So that I can smile and be fed
With His Word till I sleep on my eternal bed.

Lost Hope and Faith

Behold! Why'd I still be alive,
When to live, I no longer strive?
Why'd the Sun still shine,
Upon this poor soul of mine?

Oh! Can't anybody hear me,
Or this tattered life see?
Oh! Won't someone rescue me,
Before eternally damned I be?

Know ye not the end is near?
Know ye not, soon I won't be there?
How late find me this life so dear,
After it's consumed by tears & fear!

Here now, on the morrow ye'd search.
Too late! The casket's in the church.
Forever gone sans bidding even a bye,
Leaving ye alone to ponder on why.

(Composed as a drug addict)

Walking the Mile to Effect Smile

On the quickened wings of grace
Heaven has flown me to embrace
T'is gift of a new life, new chance;
A new music for my soul to dance.

I've buried my past dark and dreary,
Decided to live and not grow weary,
And in His confidence, play my role
O' restoring hope in a hopeless soul.

For what the rejected and lost feel
Is subtly used by t'e adversary to kill,
In one strike, both the spirit and soul
And condemn 'em to hell's fiery bowl.

I've lived so and felt the hardest blow;
Trampled down as the lowliest of low,
But I survived wit' scars to tell my tale,
To save those He's given me from hell.

In His confidence, I shall walk the mile,
Try my best to make others wear smile;
And bring 'em to the knowledge of God,
T'at they too may be free from sin's load.

The God of New Beginnings

(His Mercy Endureth Forever)

Walking along the lonely, dreary road;
Alien from the path you once trod;
Leaving behind the good guide;
Lured away to the dark side.

Knowing not where the road leads;
Ignorant of the sign that reads-
"Destination Hell" for souls
For whom the Bell tolls.

All the while the adversary smiles,
As you cover the cursed miles.
Till you discover it's too late
To escape your ugly fate.

But God does keep watch and cry
Over your soul that's gone dry.
For His mercy angels plead-
Seeking for Grace to lead.

Saints too, make their plea and pray,
For you to find back your way
Into the path o' truth and light-
To dying soul's delight!

Tear-filled prayers move the Lord,
And in His grace and His Word,
He stretches forth His Hand
Ere you turn the final bend.

Halted from your Journey to Hell,
You'd return with a Story to tell,
If only you'd give your hand
To God o' the beginning and end.

His love ends and vexes evil plans
Puts to nought dark designs
He is, for spirit grooming,
God of new beginnings!

The Voyage Continues

The sea is calm tonight.
The sky lit wit' stars bright.
My lonely Voyage continues,
Guided only by heavenly clues.

Captain of my own soul,
I'd chosen to heed the call
Of my destiny from the deep;
And I'd keep sailing ere I sleep.

Deadly storms I've faced
Had faith and hope replaced
By clouds of despair and rage;
Proved too costly for my voyage.

Anchor'd for many moons;
Idly living out cursed boons
In an island of vain pleasures.
Bartered off life's true treasures.

Wretched but still alive,
Sought the Lord to revive
The soul of a wrecked vessel,
That it may once again take sail.

Adieu, island of vanity!
I have regained my sanity.
Ye caused my sins to mature;
Robbed my age, not my future!

Thus, I bid thee farewell,
And leave wit' a tale to tell,
As I continue with my venture
That would lead me to my future.

The sea is calm tonight.
My vessel casts a sore sight.
The winds may turn unfriendly,
But I must keep on sailing bravely.

The God of "The Second Chance"

There are times when the sinners silently weep,
Finding themselves drowning, sinking deep,
In the murky waters of worldly pleasure
They once loved to swim in at leisure,
To exercise their God-given freewill,
With a choice that would only kill-
Both the mortal body and soul,
And parcel them to Sheol.

It's their heart that weeps,
Whilst the world gently sleeps.
Sin-stained dream awakens them;
Past memory only spells ugly shame;
The soul's gut-wrenching cries of protest,
O'er the envisioned Place for its eternal rest,
Keep 'em awake-wishing and longing for rescue.
But finding none they weep and weep as their due.

Sometimes their weeping' heart is seen by the Lord,
Whose love, and grace, and mercy cannot afford
To be overshadowed by the sins of the world.
Thus He chooses instead to love and scold,
And gives strength and comfort to them.
That they mayn't drown in their shame,
But for death, a new life exchange
From t'e God of 'second chance'.

Has Your Heart Grown Cold?

Has your heart grown cold?
Because of your memories old,
Or for nascent but tough situation,
That robs your peace and seek attention.

Has your heart grown cold?
Because you are no more bold,
And your enemy has an upper hand
In battles fought in your inherited land.

Has your heart grown cold?
Because of the ugly past retold
By t'ose who love to open your scar,
And know not how you'd come this far.

Has your heart grown cold?
Because you've no silver or gold;
And your soul yearns to live wealthy,
While your fatigue body turns unhealthy.

Has your heart grown cold?
Because o' dreams you can't hold;
Havin' waited patiently for a big break,
You let go easy and your system's a wreck.

Has your heart grown cold?
Because of your privileges sold-
To your foe who seeks aft'r your soul,
And desires to hold captive of one and all.

Life's happiness depends on
How you tackle life as your own;
Understanding your body as a temple,
Living simple and always remaining humble.

Amid Storms of Life

When stormy clouds of adversity
Overshadow the plan of Almighty
And cast gloom over your labour
To rob you of your joy and honour;

When despair creeps into your life
And cuts deep into hope like a knife
To leave you wounded and pleading
For mercy before you die bleeding;

When your pleas are heard by no one
And hope o' rescue seems long gone
To leave you all alone with your tears
And make you suffer all horrific fears;

When your cries evoke only laughter
From the swelling crowd that gathers
To mock at your tragedy and miseries
And bid for your soul that still tarries;

When your present raises a banner-
An ensign waving you're no winner,
And your future remains but clueless
To so mark life's journey as hopeless;

When every effort seems to go in vain
And days pass by to usher greater pain,
As darker nights spell your misfortunes
And perform t'e dirge in mournful tunes;

When agony's stream flow endless
And Hope itself seems all hopeless,
And your heart decides to give up
At the overflow of your bitter cup,

Take heart & give up not on dear life,
Though it may seem only full o' strife.
Remind your soul, "seeth the Creator",
And in His time His hand will restore.

What you feel to be utter hopelessness
Could well draw you to His faithfulness,
And mark the beginning of a life afresh-
On whom Heaven its blessings unleash.

For what's life full of misery and pain
But the very reason that He was slain,
T'at you and I may believe in the Cross
And bear no more worldly pain or loss!

So, have faith my dear, even amid storm!
God who sees to safety a wiggling worm
Would verily stretch His compassionate hand
And bring you safe across His Promised Land.

Striving on Till "Rest"

Turbulent times and situations I face,
Sometimes, slow down my race.
Discouragement raises its ugly head
And blurs my vision to go ahead.
Heaven seems to go deaf to prayers
Uttered by a soul seeking answers,
Whilst days fleet by sans consolation
And I remain under confusion.

Hark! The soft, still voice announces,
"Idle not away His gifted chances,
Or give in to the lies of the adversary,
Nor be trapped in his controversy,
God sees and, in His time, will restore
Your honour and you'd cry no more"...
Down in the dumps but kept alive,
I'll crawl back and continue to strive,
And go on living and hoping for the best
Till my earthly life comes to rest.

Plea to Complete the Race

Dear Lord, please make haste.
Let not my time go to waste.
I have run the course thus far
Carrying along my fears and scar.
In the name of Love and Grace,
Let me overcome and finish my race.

Nature spells unfavourable climes,
And troubled days I face ofttimes.
But make me understand and accept
The truth of the day and not suspect,
That others enjoy only blissful days
While I alone face the doomed rays.

Incline my ways to Your purpose,
And my wish to what You propose.
Keep me away from fears and lies,
As I desire to give a thousand tries
For the work I consider my honour;
And glory be Yours alone ever more.

The All-seeing Eye

Behold the Eye, holding the universe in it.
It watches the created from its high seat;
Unblinking from the beginning of heaven;
Observant of everything with focus even.

IT has watched the unseen Word order
Life and all things in a space of wonder,
From the birth of galaxies and planets
To single-cell organisms in sea depths.

IT has kept track of all t'at was created-
Even the forces unseen by eyes naked.
The first witness of the entire universe
As it unfolded to reveal nature diverse.

IT witnessed the fall of man in the Eden
And thereafter his life out of the garden.
IT marvelled to behold the first rainbow,
That God painted in the sky as His vow.

The witness & judge of the first murder
When envy claimed the life of a brother,
IT remains the sole Judge for all times.
It's the Eye of justice against all crimes.

The Eye that sees beyond what we see
Is the same t'at watches over you & me.
Nothing goes unnoticed under its watch.
IT follows the Word in a perfect match.

All our deeds are laid bare in its sight,
For IT sees wit' the power of the Light;
Penetrating the depths of our soul,
IT watches thought shaping into goal.

Good or bad, nothing escapes the Eye.
IT captures everything of us till we die.
IT' would act as the chief witness of all
W'en souls stand in the judgement Hall.

Behold the Eye, filled with compassion
For men and his seeds of every nation;
IT watches in patience for men to turn
From their follies, lest in hell they burn.

Lines from a Sojourner

Alone I sojourn-
Scarred and torn-
In this mortal world.
My dream still unfurled;
Blurred by past battles lost,
T'at revisit my mind like ghosts.

Tears are many;
Fewer days sunny.
My nights are longer,
Dark memories stronger.
My present hurts- it's blamed
For what dark past has claimed.

Wish t'ey knew,
Like morning dew
Vanishing in the Sun,
My life too will be gone,
When death comes calling,
And all past/present go sailing.

Till such day
Comes this way,
Alone I will sojourn,
Just t'e way I was born.
Scripting a story o' my own...
Only few would have e'er known.

Transition

Some nights, when the world's fast asleep,
And silence reigns over the darkness deep,
His thoughts struggle wit' his wish to rest,
Steal his moments like an uninvited guest
Who narrates stories o' the miserable past,
To evoke memories t'at would hold on fast.

Sad memories t'at wet his pillow at night;
Leave him weeping alone wit' spent might;
No more would he plead or care to sleep-
Lest his emotions and sanity take a leap.
Spent as he be, he'd hope for a new dawn
To help fight and keep his demons down.

As days go by, he'll conquer his fears;
No more shed those bitter silent tears,
Or allow the demons to reign or scare.
Beautiful memories through deeds fair,
Shall overwhelm his regrets and sorrows,
And peace descends on his tomorrows!

Hard Decisive Days

Days fleeting by like clouds ere the storm
Hastened by adversity in its cruellest form,
T'at eats away into the fibres of your heart,
As time flies, and a relationship falls apart.

Who'd have foreseen such an outcome
Of love waxing cold in spirits lonesome,
Of trust betrayed by ugly secrets and lies,
As the aggrieved soul inconsolably cries.

Times were when I harnessed my thought
And meddled not in bloody battles fought;
Times were when I restrained my poor self,
Bore unwarranted hurt like a victimised elf.

'Stead I sought and worked for brighter days.
That, what was made one may not part ways;
That, good sense may prevail over vain glory,
And All may find peace for their souls weary.

But alas! Past half a decade of suppressed tears,
T'is embittered soul protests and no more cares
About promises and commitments made hastily.
For all it ever cares, is for all of us to live happily.

Thus, I stand today, affirmed in His wisdom,
That The Decision was not made in random.
Rather in t'e knowledge of w'at was revealed
By God of w'at had long remained concealed.

And so, as my days go passing by,
My mind keeps on wondering why
God chose yours truly, who has nothing
To stand for those who have everything.

Ere the Sun go down on this life,
What now cuts deep like a knife,
Will no longer cause hurt to us;
For this too shall come to pass.

Be the Change

So, you wanna see the world change?
Maybe you, yourself gotta rearrange
Certain things in your own life first,
Like giving up on your selfish thirst.

Then you'd try to change your family:
Bring each member around gradually;
Inculcate life's principles firm and bold;
And you would've changed your world!

Then you'd try to change your friends:
Coax 'em gently outta worldly trends;
Be their guide, support and inspiration;
Make Change their goal and aspiration.

Then, with change among brotherhood,
You'd have changed the neighbourhood
Where happy, smiling faces would meet;
And peace would prevail in every street.

The Silence of the Committed

In a Land where truth is silenced,
And lies and dishonesty reign supreme;
In societies where tax is licensed,
For motherland whose future's but grim.

Across the streets painted corrupt-red,
Where lurks shadowy evil with its ugly head;
In the high echelon of government offices,
Where responsible men breed dark practices.

Amongst organisations harping for a change,
Lo! The Committed falling out o' wisdom's range,
Choosing to breathe silently in the corrupt air.
Woe betide our ways that're no more true or fair!

O God, from this land shorn of virtues o' old,
Awaken leaders and youth, honest and bold,
That'd lead us wit' wisdom & dedication,
And make our society free o' corruption.

Finding Your Way Back Into Love

Works of your adversary makes you depressed.
Looking at your own life, you are not impressed.
Your heart beats to the tune o' a mournful song;
You wonder where it could have gone all wrong...

Memories of the past make you sad;
Your scars never make you feel glad;
The present reminds you of sorrows;
Uncertainty shrouds your tomorrows.

You wish to give up and simply disappear.
Nothing, with your grief, you can compare.
Happiness seems quite out of your reach.
Your soul cries out to Him to lead and teach.

He hears your agonising cries and smiles.
He has seen you tread those lonely miles.
He reaches out and wipes away your tears,
And says "My child, leave to Me your cares."

You realise you should've sought Him earlier,
For you find your heart lifted, your life dearer.
Finding your way back into His Arms of Love,
You smile and sing praises to Heaven above.

Come Home

(Return, Ye Prodigal Son!)

Drifting away from the Shepherd's fold.
Treading a defiant path, lonely and cold.
Seeking but finding not what ye seek...
Turning away from truth; turning weak.

Burdened by life's toils and cares.
Revisited by past miseries and fears.
Feeling utter pain of same old scars.
Fighting lone losing battles and wars.

Unheeding to the voice of a weeping soul.
Ignorant to the Shepherd's relentless call.
Deaf to the music t'at plays "come home".
Blind amongst the evils that freely roam.

All the while the inviting music plays.
All alone dear Mama cries and prays.
Home's grown gloomy as her tears run...
Forlorn she longs for her son to return.

Fight the Good Fight;
Run the Good Race

The race, your race isn't yet over my dear,
Though your adversary has stirred up fear
Within your vexed heart to make believe
That you no longer have a purpose to live.

How oft' you forget, oh my forgetful child!
To listen to that voice- soft, tender and mild,
That small stilled voice o' your achy heart
Urgin' you to keep the faith from the start.

Son, I alone am the Author of every race,
And I desire of you to end yours in grace.
Yet, lost in pursuit of aim seemingly great,
You have lost sight of your course ahead.

Thus, the many battles you've fought.
All alone and all in your heavy thought.
Some you have won; others you lost.
And your Time has suffered the cost.

If only you had a little more patience
To go along wit' your clear conscience.
If only you'd reserved a little more faith
And let me wield t'e sword in your fight.

But for a moment, the battle seems over.
Rest your thought and regain your power
That when tomorrow wakes up its demon,
You shall be ready to fight, and have it won.

Fight the good fight my dear son;
Run the good race as days go on.
Unto you be the deserved victory.
Your head be crowned with glory.

In and With the Lord

She walks with her Lord every day;
Allows Him to lead her all the way;
E'er so gently He leads in quietude,
As she follows wit' humble attitude.

Their path leads to the golden shore;
Sparkling waters kissing the sky azure;
Clouds wave greetings as they roll by,
While t'e waters flagellate as froths fly.

In t'e vast ocean of His loving grace,
The waters of Love clean every trace
Of remnant sin from man's first Fall,
That she remains worthy of His call.

She explores the depth of the deep blue;
Marvels at the sight of life in chimeric hue,
Learns to admire and glean precious lesson
Of faith and truth lived and guided by vision.

Oh, how humbling to walk with the Lord;
To listen and inculcate values of His word!
What bliss to swim in the sea of His love,
And rest away safe and secure in His cove!

Effecting Change

Precious days go fleeting by,
And I keep wondering why
God should love me so much
Despite me losing touch
With Him and His only Son
Who ne'er leaves me alone.

Watching the Sun go down,
I go searching for what I'd own
From the day that's gone by;
And all I find is the need to try-
Try and keep trying till the end;
Believing in works of His Hand.

Mama dear taught me well:
Of this privilege to tell my tale
To those lost and heartbroken,
That they too might be forgiven;
Find their way back home;
Ere prey of Satan they become.

So, as imperfect as I am,
I try not to remain the same
In my own shell of past.
But remove self from the cast,
And perform my given role
Towards others and for my soul.

That they, too, would discover-
"Nothing in this life is over,
Nor our obligations and servitude"
Maintaining godly attitude,
If only you'd live by His principles,
You'd be His blessed disciple.

Sow the Seed of Love

Sow the seed of love,
Nurture it with faith in Heaven above,
Protect with earnest prayers,
Watch it grow into lovely flowers
Spreading forth sweet fragrance
To create beautiful remembrance;
As in days of old,
When love reigned bold
Over hatred amongst brothers
And brought them together
In spirit of oneness,
Dispelling differences.

Seeds of love more precious than gold
In hearts of men that have grown cold
To wisdom, truth and reason
Shall, in due time and season,
Spring forth tender buds of joy
And give thee reasons to enjoy;
As life blossoms into its splendid best-
Having overcome with love every test,
Ready to take a leap into future unknown,
Confident of the reward for w'at ye'd sown.

Wasted Years

As the Sun sets in the far west,
And all-day labour's put to rest,
Ponder thou on the wasted years,
On times submerged in sad tears...

Years squandered on reckless living,
Ignorant of the soul that was dying;
Years bartered for worldly pleasures,
Forsaking all the heavenly treasures.

In foolish pursuit of fleeting happiness,
Forgot thou about bitter consequences.
Drowning heaven gifted talents in vices,
Too late was it when ye came to senses.

Narrow vision betrayed precious life,
Foresee hazy future filled with strife.
Cast distant from all near and dear;
And there be none who'd e'en care.

Dear life, if only it profiteth to weep,
Over thy follies that none careth keep;
Then ye would cry a thousand river,
And stil' seek no cause from the Giver.

But alas! Nothing now would bring back
What ye'd allowed the dark past to take;
Nor could ye bring solace today,
For all that ye wasted yesterday!

The Revelatory Speaker

(Dedicated to Papa Maurice Wylie)

He treads the path that leads to the Light.
The path's strait and narrow but is lit bright.
Quite distinct from the path he once trod,
Only few have chosen to follow this road.

He bears a unique testimony of the Light;
Interprets the Word unto heaven's delight;
Preaches naught but the truth of the Word,
Lest he offend his Master who is the Lord.

Hidden truths of God's Word, he reveals.
Brings to light what the Script conceals,
That all those privileged to hear and read
May understand and profit from his lead.

In partnership with the God of the Universe,
Wit' whom he's been honoured to converse,
He sows seeds of wisdom in people's mind
That they may learn blessings of godly kind.

Multitudes treading the dark and easy path,
Turnabout to listen and desire to take bath
From the sea of revealed truths, and be clean
From all their past lies, and to the truth lean.

His banner of truth unfurled in Zion's Hill,
He continues to tread the path in HIS will.
He is subjected only to his beloved Maker.
He is God's Writer and Revelatory Speaker.

Heaven's Little Rosebud

(Dedicated to Mama's granddaughter, Amber-Rose)

There is a Heaven's little rose-bud I adore.
Precious and unique I love her to the core.
Fairest of all the lovely buds in the Garden;
She spells beauty like the first rose o' Eden.

Green-cloaked lithe body on a stalk slender.
Lo, her tiny pink head poppin' out in wonder-
Soakin' up the life-sustaining gracious Light;
Channelling purity to petals embraced tight.

How she loves to dance wit' the master wind
Who teaches her "steps of captivating kind";
Coaxing her lithesome figure to tap and sway,
Whilst she grows unhindered night and day.

Unbeknown to her pretty budding self,
She is perfected for the King Himself.
For that day when she'd receive a call
To perform in The Great Dancing Hall.

Angels on high watch o'er her constant.
Blest mortals like me from land distant
Send love and grace on wings o' prayer,
As she opens her petals layer aft'r layer.

Let no force or beast steal her innocence,
Nor any dark practice dilute her fragrance.
Instead, let her grow and bloom free and fair,
And be a source of Hope to all- far and near.

My Beloved Mum

(Ino Kimiye Chekiu IZA)

I hear her voice, soothing and tender;
At times admonishing but with care.
I watch and admire her beautiful face
Carved out from the bosom of Grace.

She loves me thro' all my highs and lows.
How much I love her only heaven knows!
She is the epitome of love unblemished;
Sacrifice and love she offers undiminished.

Ever present to support like a true friend;
How I'd do sans her I can't comprehend.
With her no problem is too hard to solve;
From her flows the fountain of God's love.

She is the wind beneath my tired wings;
Pushing me on to face what life brings.
Her presence offers strength and comfort.
No force of adversity, her teachings distort.

Angels on high gladly sing her praises.
The banner of Hope she herself raises.
She is my Queen, so full of life and grace-
The best Mum in the entire human race.

An Angel in Disguise

Time was when I had none to call my own.
Grievous it was to have my name known.
All I had were tears but couldn't cry;
And beaten wings that I couldn't fly.

Then along she came and promised hope-
The only thing I trusted and looked to cope,
With times cruel and savage to my existence;
With life survived thro' heaven's providence.

She clothed herself with love and grace.
Over my past follies a tight embrace-
To rein in every haunting memory,
To lull vices with hope-filled story.

Upon her honour, she carried my name;
Taught me ways to redeem my shame.
Of the future, she envisioned paradise.
Coaxed my stunted will to boldly arise.

Times were when I had horrendous dreams,
And pierced the night with muffled screams.
Till she poured her own dreams into mine,
And let me escape with her on cloud nine.

She is my Angel sent from the Heaven;
Come with love to make my past even.
An ever presence in every dark season
She'll, one day, take me to her mansion.

Song of a Freed Soul

(Alone, But Never Lonely)

Alone she frolics with the happy flowers-
Beauties t'at have no owner nor growers.
Dancing to the rhythm of the blooming wild,
As the wind teases her tresses and dress mild.

Above the sky watches her tryst with nature,
As she sings unmindful o' the past or future-
A song echoed through yonder valleys aloud,
And joyously absorbed by the looming cloud.

Hers is a song sung by those with a pure heart;
A melody-sweet and captivating from the start,
With lyrics inspired & penned by a soul set free.
Hers is a song that gladly beckons you and me!

Mother - The Sweetest Name of All

Mother! The name itself, so sweet to hear;
The high and the low, honour her so dear;
The most Holy knew He couldn't be near
In person, He placed mothers everywhere!

So came Mother to take care of our world,
And of its men of every race, freed or sold,
With qualities God himself engraved in her,
That men may marvel & glorify God in fear.

So entered mothers in every home,
Beautiful creatures in human form;
Unique, with love so gentle and pure;
Strength, at all times, great to endure.

A daughter once, she understands children,
Guides them with care, and in wisdom train,
And for their happiness walk the extra mile,
That they may always think o' her and smile.

As wife, a faithful soulmate o' her husband,
With a bigger heart & stronger hands to lend.
Patience's her fortress, t'ere she stands tall,
For her family ever ready to sacrifice her all!

The Lonely Widow

Alone, she feels lost and lonely.
The Sun for her has set too early.
Ere remembered by all so fondly,
Here she misses company dearly.

The cold, icy wind of winter
Freezes her memories bitter
Of that dark day last summer
When death claimed her lover.

Seasons had passed, still remains fear;
April showers reminds her grief to bear.
In her deluded mind left utterly bare,
E'ery raindrop's mothered by her tear.

Autumn evokes in her mind o' emptiness,
As she pines for his care and closeness.
Spring buds forth into solitariness;
As sorrows bloom into emptiness.

Her days pass in mournful tears;
Her nights filled with nightmares-
Of miseries which she alone bears,
Of future with all its toils and cares.

Lo! Death tolls no bell of joy or gain,
But she'd learn to take flight again.
For dark death, nor sunshine, or rain
Shall claim the grace which remains.

Finish the Race... with Grace

Trying to run and hide away;
Losing hope every other day;
Shying from responsibilities;
Escaping from hard realities...

But dear soul, you started the war,
Make efforts now to bring peace.
You also sowed the seed of hatred,
Why can't you sow the seed of love?

Don't walk away so far,
Bearing only that scar...
Taking all wounds in your flight,
Pretending everything is alright.

Be a man, O my dear!
Succumb not to fear!
Return home and finish your race,
While there's still enough o' grace.

When Hope Seems Lost

When hope seems lost but there's none to care;
When sorrow overwhelms, and constant is fear;
When tears are many, but cries heard by none;
When friends disappear, leaving you all alone...

When answers are few, but many the questions;
When doubt vexes the purpose of your creation;
When you're made to drink from the bitter cup,
And you say, "enough is enough, I'm giving up!"

Remember, there is someone who cares
Who understands your sorrows and fears,
Waits patiently to wipe away your tears;
Ready to fill your cup with joyful cheers....

He's a God who gave you a place on Earth,
He knows everything about you from birth.
With blessings and hope He silently waits,
For you to search Him in prayer and faith.

Like a Flower in a Barren Land

(To Little Children)

Like sunshine peeping out from clouds;
Like flowers blooming in a barren land-
You, children, are reason we hope aloud
And trust in to bring change in our land.

Grow well, in time, to usher in your reign
Wit' a revolutionary banner as an ensign.
Give not into the pressure of your elders-
Who's grown to follow the worldly orders.

Keep t'e faith on God who made you,
And He shall bless and guide you too.
Heed not to t'e voice o' t'e adversary,
Nor indulge thy mind in controversy.

You're tomorrow's leaders; our very future.
Bloom as rare flowers in bosom of nature.
Spread your lovely fragrance far and wide;
T'e future is all for you to take and decide.

Child O' Hope and Light

Behold the light, a child carry
In her innocent life, as she tarries
In this world of deceiving darkness;
'Tis a beacon of hope for the hopeless.

Let no dark angel, beast or man;
Let no divining spirit nor evil omen
Wax strong against her lonely sojourn.
'Stead, to protect her may we've it sworn.

Hope she carries in her breast
Is one on which all our hopes rest.
Innocence and pureness in her fold,
Incense to renew the souls grown cold.

Make way for her safe passage!
Let no beastly force defile her age.
For w'en we hurt and brin' her sorrow,
We will have no hope for our tomorrow.

Have Faith

Have faith my dear,
Give up not to fear,
Nor to insecurities of life,
Or to hard reality of strife.

Have faith: The Sun will shine
Upon your sad life and mine,
Though harsh our lot might be today;
Soon all our tears will be wiped away.

Heaven takes no pleasure in sorrow,
But desires to help poor souls grow;
Gives a chance to make a fresh start,
To heal and mend every broken heart.

Why Worry?

Don't worry for your future needs,
Nor punish 'self for past misdeeds.
They would only bring you sorrow,
And cause your anxieties to grow.

Bother not about what to wear or eat,
Nor go fidgeting in your comfy seat.
Let all your regrets turn into lessons,
Nothing occurs without some reasons.

Don't worry about tomorrow
Judiciously use today to sow
The seeds of kindness and love.
Entrust t'e rest to heaven above.

Each day brings troubles of its own;
Some, the fruits of what ye'd sown
In the irresponsible past of banalities,
That vex your mind with uncertainties.

Unconsoled Tears

Unconsoled tears of a lonely soul,
Left alone to answer miseries' call.
Groping in the emptiness of heart
For a space to set sorrows apart.

Every teardrop a reminder of pain,
Over humble efforts gone in vain.
Every breathe an extension of grief,
Over misfortunes hoped to be brief.

Gathered on pillow every lonely night;
Tears and thoughts deprived of light.
Left to suffer agony even in dreams;
Where tears flow in endless streams.

Love was When...

Love was when you realised, she was lost:
Abandoned by all others at sorrow's coast,
Took her into your bosom and sailed away
Yonder to your island where happiness lay.

Love was when you read into her mind,
And divined she was of a different kind-
Ignorant in ways and manners of t'e world,
But willing to learn, and beautiful and bold.

Love was when you first kissed her,
And she reciprocated as would a lover.
But restrained from taking It further,
Lest she displease the eternal Father.

Love was when you wiped away her tears,
And with your kisses, melted all her fears,
With your hugs, warmed her icy-cold heart,
With your smile, gave hope for a new start.

Love was when your word spelled comfort;
Your confidence and trust- her strong Fort;
Your chastening- wonderful lessons of life,
And your ambitions-hope to bear any strife.

Why, oh why did you let your love rust away,
For vain glories, and for the games you play?
Was it a lie when you first pleaded 'I love you'?
And coaxed her later to say, "I love you too"?

Give Me Wings

Give me the wings to fly;
Not be the reason to cry.
Give me my share of joy;
Never play me like a toy.

Give me my voice to say;
Like a man living his way.
Give me a space to live;
And Life's best I'd give.

Give me a reason to smile;
And I'll walk another mile.
Give me a chance to dream;
And I'll flow in your stream.

Give me the purpose to exist;
And none to my approach resist.
Give me the means to celebrate;
No more tragedies I'd recreate.

Life's best surprise glows,
When time eternal flows.
To give chance to impoverished.
That his life could be cherished.

Born to Fly

Spread your wings, Love,
And soar in skies above.
Wipe your sad tears dry,
And up away happily fly.

Let not the world hold you back,
Nor men cause your will t' slack.
In the strength of your innocence,
May you realize joy in abundance.

Worry not, world has always been
For the morrow eyes haven't seen.
Just keep the faith and keep flying
To rescue your dream that's dying.

Ere the day's over to usher in night,
Take t' higher reach your solo flight.
Let the hope t'at in your heart rings
Be the wind underneath your wings.

Release your doubts and cares,
That often give you nightmares.
Merge free with Mother nature;
She'd guide you t' better future.

When your wings grow weary,
And heart goes faint and dreary,
And no longer you wish to try-
Remember, you're born to fly!

Racing Against Time?

As days go rushing by,
I keep wondering why
Man always keeps himself busy
And never learn to take life easy.

He quickens his age,
But fills not his page,
Nor paints his canvas God offers;
He races 'gainst time and suffers.

In the name of peoples in strife,
In the name of ambitions of life,
He pursues windblown pleasure
And loses the pure fun of leisure.

Life comes and goes;
And what a man does
Comes to naught if it's not done
As purposed long ere he is gone.

To race against time,
It'd amount to crime;
For time shall pass on to eternity,
But a man will die with his vanity.

Stop a while, take time to listen!
Why t'is gift of life do ye hasten?
Why race away and reap sorrow,
W'en uncertain is your tomorrow?

Life Continues

Empty Room, depressed Mind,
Tears of the inconsolable kind;
Cries from the aggrieved heart,
Bearing burden of mindful hurt.

Poor Soul, it pours when it rains for me.
Presenting a blurred vision of w'at I see.
Makes me wonder what life is all about-
If it's worth all the battles I have fought!

Hark! God isn't an author of confusion.
He, in Grace, lords over every situation.
He'll never burden you with such a load,
T'at'd stall your journey in t'e strait road.

Thus, with this flickering Light of mine
I tread on, ever cautious of the redline;
Battling with my demons each new day,
Gleaning lessons in every possible way.

Challenges and temptations in all forms,
Keep pressing hard beyond all norms;
At times, too great a problem to bear,
For this lonely soul with none to care.

Yet, to God be given glory that is due,
As this lone journey of life continues.
No matter what my adversary brings,
May I face it boldly as my soul sings.

Soul Children of my Dream

I saw a child:
Eyes as beguiled,
Escaping gaze in fear;
Clothed in a clumsy wear;
Matt'd hair on oversiz'd head,
Hung on shoulders droopin' sad.
I asked, "who be ye and where goeth?"
He said, "I am a soul child of t'e curseth;
Fathered by greedy and corrupt leaders.
I goeth where the condemned lot gathers!"

I saw another child:
Eyes cold-red and wild;
Rash voice that stuttered;
His body, hurt and battered,
Blood oozing from cut wound;
Helplessly stretch'd on a ground.
I asked, "Who be ye and how hurteth?"
He said, "I'm a soul-child of t'e curseth;
Fathered by rapists, killers and murderers.
My wounds reflect hurt they inflict on others."

I saw another child:
Eyes cast happy mild;
Dressed in a lovely attire;
Dancing around with a lyre,
Singing a song of joy and love,
Melodious strain like from above.
I asked, "Who be ye and why rejoiceth?"
He said, "I am a soul-child of the blesseth;
Fathered by honest and God-fearing people.
I rejoice, for theirs is home in heaven eternal."

Dreams and Aspirations

Oh, to escape into quietude and peace,
Where every sorrow and care cease.

To have freedom in its entirety,
And be shorn of every cruelty.

To bask under the Sun o' equality,
And toil with smiles to eternity.

To dream away in happy slumber,
And have no worries to remember.

To love and be loved always,
And be perfected in all ways.

To be Light in someone's darkness,
And evoke truth and all goodness.

Oh! To aspire for higher living,
The world says, I'm dreaming!

My Winter Sonnet

The winter with its numbing wind and cold
Makes me feel I have grown just too old-
Lazy and longing for the warmth of summer;
Phobic to bath and bite o' unheated water.

Short-lived be a hot shower's pleasure-
Like sweet lovers' lips locked in leisure;
Forced apart by time in all suddenness-
As unforgiving cold hugs my nakedness.

But O! The memories & lessons of Winter-
Must I forget in the cruel heat of Summer?
Surely, the heavens had blessed this season.
And live I must, in accordance to the reason.

My youth like t'e season won't last forever.
Come Spring, I hope, I'd grow a little wiser.

Why, oh Why?

Why do the mortals live in laxity
And barter their years for vanity?
Why do mankind live in disparity
When we could all live in unity?

Why do men lose their integrity
In vain search of famed identity?
Why do we suffer dire poverty
When we can live in prosperity?

Why do crimes recur in a community
When Law is in force in every society?
Why do men and women lose sanity
And reap upon themselves a penalty?

Why do churches preach o' quantity
When Heaven searches for quality?
Why does a leader ignore his duty
And let his followers suffer cruelty?

Why do politicians seek luxury and fame
And gobble the poor's share sans shame?
Why do criminals stage crime like a game
And later live their lives cloak'd wit' blame?

Why do rich men hoard riches and wealth
But ignore heaven's treasures, and health?
Why're beggars' cries and tears hardly felt
By 'em who laugh to have t'eir hearts melt?

Why, Oh why? This soul keeps asking why.
But the answers may never come ere I die.
Yet so long as t'e Sun shines for me, I'll try
To get t'e answers till 'tis time for goodbye.

Vanity of vanities!
Life of banalities!
How could we give ourselves to stupidity
And lose our world, our souls for eternity?

The Voice

Across the God-gifted Land of Nagas,
Replete with history of a bloody saga,
An enraged voice echoes in the valleys,
Reverberating in the streets and alleys.

'Tis the voice of young men and women:
Longing to flee from corrupts' domain;
Crying out to heavens for deliverance
From dishonest men and their influence.

'Tis the voice of a betrayed generation:
Dreaming of an early peaceful solution,
For a Cause fathered by score o' leaders-
Each wit' a motley crew of tax gatherers.

'Tis the voice of faithful believers:
Praying for God-inspired preachers
To wax strong amongst poor or rich;
Live according to what they preach!

'Tis the voice of innocent children:
Beseeching to lighten their burden,
Made heavier by the ignorant elders;
More unbearable by corrupt leaders!

Deaf to the ears of the unrepentant,
The voice soaked in tearful content
Resonates in the Heaven's corridor,
And seek justice for every corruptor!

The ever-patient God has watched
The responsible evils go untouched,
But He'll curse and vex every corrupt's way
And raise an honest generation on His day!

Youths of Our Time

Behold the youths, in their golden years
Living on their parent's sweat and tears;
Ignorant of the precious days fleetin' by;
Hectic routine to reason or question why.
Multitudes have gone astray or got lost
In pursuit of worldly pleasure at all cost.
Few remember and follow the teaching
Of the parents, elders and their preaching.

Dumb and deaf to the beckoning of future,
Bartering away their ambition in leisure,
Theirs is a life full of dreams and hope,
Sans the knowledge to realise and cope
With the times that herald their entrance
Into this world t'at seems to be in trance.

Vanity

Watching the world through my window,
Life seems like a dream; man, a shadow.
Days pass by like clouds in skies azure-
Swept by winds of change at its leisure.

Floating in the air of our vexed dreams;
Reality rushing away like busy streams;
The mortal flesh but lives on confused.
Precious pages of life remain unused.

The world has learned to walk in sleep.
Lessons of eternity, men failed to keep.
Living for pleasure, an iconic standard.
Many have strayed, hearts grown hard.

Oh, the vanities of a debased mankind!
Seeking after treasures you'd ne'er find.
Ruled over by the rulers of dark forces,
Thoughts have been enslaved by vices.

If only the world had wisdom of ages,
It would script history's grand pages
With deeds of man akin to God's love
And save itself the wrath from above.

Lamentation

(Nagaland Roads)

To the honour of our politicians great,
To the credit of t'eir wealth and estates,
To the name and fame of bureaucrats:
Behold, our Roads, in deplorable state!

Salute to our Secretaries and Directors!
Bravo! Ye selfish and shrewd contractors,
Praises be to the Head of Departments:
T'eir power and riches are to us torment!

Woe be to them who live for themselves,
And to worldly pleasure become slaves;
Peace and real joy elude t'eir glitzy lives;
While sorrow to t'eir vex-hearts cleaves.

Thousands fooled by one corrupt leader,
With promises of Change and life better.
Arise, Nagas! Our past and present reveal
And plead us to make a favourable deal.

Come the inevitable time for a change,
Nagas would have learnt to rearrange;
And no more make the same mistake
'Stead elect leaders for common sake!

Here I Am!

Here I am oh, the Great I AM!
As imperfect as I am,
Let me desire to bear Thy holy name
And not seek after wealth or fame.

Here I am, oh, gracious Lord.
Let me live according to Thy Word,
And wield IT as a double-edged sword
To cut free any evil harnessing cord.

Here I am, oh eternal Father,
Waiting for Thee to deliver
This soul from any dark power,
That I may always be Yours forever.

Here I am, Lord Saviour.
Thy presence I seek in every hour,
That I may continue to savour
Thy gift of love granted in my favour.

Here I am, oh, God in the highest.
Let not this striving spirit rest
Until it has gone through every test,
And earned its reward for doing its best.

Here I am, oh God of all seasons.
Cleanse and use me for good reasons,
That precious souls in dark prisons
May find way back into your mansions.

Here I am, oh God of goodwill.
Fill your love in this Dancing Quill,
So, it dances according to Thy will
And grace other souls with loving thrill.

Here I am, oh the Great I AM.
Take me just as I am.
Refine my ways for the sake of Thy name;
And of Thy love, let this soul proclaim.

Dream Lesson

She wakes up with a fright
In the dead of the night.
Perspiring profusely,
Shaken so visibly.

Clutching her blanket tight,
She switches on the light.
As her dreams unfold,
Her heart goes cold.

She saw herself in her dream,
Unable to shout or scream,
As she in thin air floated
Above her body dead.

Covered from head to toe,
'twas kept in the morgue.
She watched in horror,
As two nurses enter.

They chatted away sans care.
Like feelingless robot-pair.
Saying, "The dead's face
Reveals evil or grace".

"Depending on deeds and thought,
How ye fared in battles fought,
What ye accomplished/lost
In one's lifetime as host".

The floating spirit on hearing so
Became too curious to know,
And see how she looked
As per how she worked.

She glided down to her corpse;
Stood behind the elder nurse,
Who pulled away the sheet...
The flesh and spirit meet.

And lo, the spirit nearly fainted!
For her face was so evil-rated,
With scars and pus-filled sore,
Unmasking the life o' a whore.

Reminded of her dark profession,
That'd only spell own destruction,
She decided to start living clean,
And on faith, hope and love lean.

Realisation

My restless, clumsy haired-head aches;
My trust-betrayed heart painfully takes
The onus of blame that rings in the air,
And haunts my life constantly wit' fear.
Dark a moonless night could've drawn,
And my hard day's labour would drown
In the deep waters o' painful memories
Only to evaporate in the air of reveries.

How I wish I'd drank the potion of love
From the Cup offered by Heaven above
Ere the Sun & the moon had grown dim
To vex my ambition and blur my dream.
How I wish I'd accepted the truth earlier,
And spent my days in ways much better;
But God stil' does gift me a new morning,
That I may live on with a fresh beginning.

Before I Am Gone

Before I am gone, and am no more,
Hear, O God, this plea I humbly pour;
Cast not Thy eyes on my past iniquities,
Nor on my years lost to selfish vanities.

Before I am gone, and am no more,
Look, O God, at the lonely sojourner.
Unlike Faithful, I've ofttimes strayed,
But to journey in truth I've also prayed.

Before I am gone, and am no more,
Touch, O God, this heart's sad core;
Beating away in mournful rhythms,
Longing to sing your holy anthems.

Before I am gone, and am no more,
Heal, O God, this ever mindful sore,
Eating away into health and conscience.
Let sense prevail over every ignorance!

Grace, Mercy and Love

(Heaven's Triplet Blessings)

Looking through the prism of life gone by,
What my eyes see makes me wonder why
God's grace continues to pour into my soul
Even though I failed to enact my given role.

I painted no rainbows in His skies,
Instead pained His heart with lies-
My lies that ruined His gifted canvas
With grey sketches that my life was.

But the merciful God says, "That was yesterday,
And what really matters is My gift to ye of today,
That is given ye out of my goodness and favour.
So ye may still paint My skies in myriad colours."

And soaking up His blessings of the Triplet
Of grace, mercy and love, I tread on and let
Him guide me through life's every rough bend,
Till, in His Time, my journey comes to an end.

Thoughts in Lines and Rhymes

Memory of the old past,
Carry only if it is a must.
Hold onto the truth fast;
Lies turn mind into rust.

Leave hurt to the Lord.
Meditate on His Word.
Wrongs, do not record;
Tears, you can't afford.

Leave to the Lord revenge.
It is not prudent to avenge.
Pray for Love to rearrange
Things you cannot change.

Lies and truth sits not in the same row;
Liar from your company out you throw.
Lies and deceptions reward you sorrow;
Truth lights the path to a better morrow.

Hearken to what the still soft voice says,
Of tribulations and trials in the last days.
Be sufficiently prepared in all your ways
Grace may not be there for thee always.

The Stream of my Dream

I saw a stream
In my dream.
From its source
It flowed with force.
Nothing on its path dare detain,
Nor the Bowls of earth retain
All o' its crystal-clear water.
The Bowls did gather,
But they couldn't contain
All the waters up in the Mountain.
Pools after pools it formed-
Large and small, round and deformed.

The over spilling waters
Carried all decayed matters,
And flowed away a gentle stream
Filling every empty space up to brim.
The Stream livened up plants and trees;
And receiving other tributaries
It turned into a mighty river,
Coursing the whole o' land in power,
To finally meet and merge with the sea.
And no more was I allowed to see!

I heard a Voice.
It said "Rejoice!"
"The outpouring of God's love
Is like the waters from high above,
That cascade down to form a stream,
Like crystal-clear waters of your dream.
No dark force dare plug its source,
Nor any mortal change its course.

It graces every dry, empty heart.
Reviving 'em to make a fresh start
By washing their sins away.
That they may live happy and gay;
That their deeds, in Heaven, be treasured
And their souls, of salvation, rest assured.

Letting Go

The night is calm and still.
High atop a lush green hill
An old church bell chimes,
As she scripts her rhymes.

Winter's on, draped in cold.
Absorbed in her own world
She reminisces about past,
That forever seems to last.

She paints a true love story,
That now remains a history
For lovers to read and learn
When to let go & take a turn.

Words flow free like a stream,
As she remembers her dream
Of a bright future wit' her lover
Who'd be both a taker & a giver.

It was only a winter moon ago;
He avowed never to let her go,
But live life for the sake of love,
And be one in the realm above.

W'en Spring swept away Winter,
Nothing else seemed to matter,
Save the greatest day in her life
W'en she was to become a wife.

Soon she prepared for marriage,
Careless of the difference in age-
He, her lover, a decade year older
But to her age really didn't matter.

Lost deep, dreaming of her future,
It was devastating when love pure
Was abruptly taken away to grave,
And she could do nothing to save.

Her belief and hopes came to halt,
And she lived in ways she best felt.
Winter came & memory swept over
The times she shared wit' her lover.

Months after months passed by,
And finally, she decided not to cry.
Instead to move on she would try
And stop asking God 'just so why'

And deep in the atrium of her heart
She will herself to make a new start,
And thus, she scripts her love story,
T'at she'll live and to God give glory.

Her story began in hot summer,
Stamped it closed in the winter
To accept her fate and make turn
And not allow her heart to burn.

The night is calm and still.
High atop a lush green Hill,
Children in the church sing;
She joins to praise the King.

Tears for Scars

Shedding tears for the scars of the past;
But you know that memories won't last.
Still you keep crying out miserable tears
And get entrapped in the midst of fears...
When you're coming out from the shell,
Only those who really understand well
Care to wish you the best and comfort,
And stand up for you like a strong fort,
Keeping you under their wings of prayer
To make you feel counted and secure.
All in accordance to Heaven's will,
That life's purpose maybe fulfilled.

My tears dry up, and I am not crying anymore,
Instead, I'll live in Him who lives for evermore.

Share

Lost to selfish ways of the world,
In pursuit of fame, name and gold.
Forgot the wise words of the old;
Ignorant of what mother had told.

Not a dime or a substance to share,
Nor a moment for the poor to care.
Ever busy for life that seems unfair;
Holding onto amassed riches dear.

Surely, ye'd at least spare some love,
As freely as ye received from above.
Surely, ye'd at least smile and prove
That life's best gifts lie not in trove.

Alas! Ye had always been a hoarder
O' things that rot and to dust gather.
Promise today if ye will to be a giver,
And see this world change for better!

Wait no longer for a season or a day,
Nor bother for what others might say;
But begin to share what ye'd this day,
That others too remain happy and gay.

Our Family Cemetery

I paid a visit to our family cemetery;
A row of tombs in perfect symmetry;
Rest home sans exit under the trees.
Here lieth dear ones; their souls free.

Signature of death on each tombstone,
Certifying the passing on of loved one.
Epitaphs relating stories in a grim tone,
Of late beloveds God chose to be gone.

They will never pass again this way,
But come my heaven appointed day,
I will get rested where I stand today,
And my spirit takes their lead, I pray!

This world is but one global cemetery.
The rich and poor, the bond and free;
All shall pass thro' and none escape,
When death recalls our time on its lap.

Over the mountains, across the valleys;
In the deserts, and seas, and our alleys.
The mortal remains thus testify,
'In death dost all mankind unify'

To live and to die is but once.
Death gifts none a chance.
From ashes we have risen;
To ashes we will turn again.

The Place I Know to be Heaven

Far away from the world of vanities
Is a place reserved for all eternities;
Where your heart remains satisfied,
And your mind, liberated & edified.

'Tis a place where hope rings true.
No tempest trouble its ocean blue,
Nor sorrow cast its gloomy shadows
O'er peace-graced hills and meadows.

Lit'le children frolic under the golden Sun,
As the air fills with their laughter and fun.
Young people roam the street sans fear,
While elders walk unaided in happy pairs.

'Tis a place that sees no rot or decay-
Where life stages one continuous play,
And the actors enact their saintly roles
In the great theatre o' redeemed souls.

'Tis a place where hosts of angels sing
In melodious strain the glory o' the King;
And wit' all souls worship in one accord
The holiest of the Holy- the Saviour Lord!

Past the hectic life of mortal toils & cares,
When the righteous have shed their tears,
The glorious dawn shall usher in all the chosen
To this paradisiacal home I know to be Heaven.

Ode to Asu Isak Chishi Swu

Darkness spreads o'er the valleys;
Silent goes the streets and alleys;
Gloomy clouds rest on mountains;
Tears flow like mournful fountains...

Skies azure shed raindrops of sorrow,
Pierced by sunbeams to cast rainbow;
Birds sing tearful melodies in misty air,
As God recalls His chosen just and fair.

Behold the land's beloved on his day,
He puts his armour and mantle away
To end a chapter scripted with his life-
Sacrificed to free our lives from strife.

The Land has never stood so still,
O'er a void only Heaven could fill...
For the leader put to gentle sleep,
Thousands awake in silence weep.

In life, you walked the path of sacrifice;
Left a legacy to be emulated in demise.
Your journey ends, Oh Asü, beloved leader!
But your cause and memory will live forever.

For a Meaningful Living

During the mortals' probationary life
In this hectic world filled with strife,
Help ease thy brethren's load,
As you tread the narrow road.

Lighter is the burden to carry,
And lesser be reasons to worry
When a helping hand is offered
To those who grieve and suffer.

Pay heed to wise advices;
Surrender not to your vices,
Or to temptations of any kind,
Nor entertain evil in your mind.

The purer the thought,
The better your growth;
The cleaner the wealth,
The dearer your health.

Humble be your ways,
More your sunny days.
Duty be your passion,
Noble your aspiration.

Take care and do well to remember
To keep love in thy heart's chamber;
And share what you are blessed with
To those God purposed you to meet.

The Bird Has Flown

The bird has flown!
But oh, I didn't own,
Nor could I care enough,
Wit' my nature so rough.

I've foolishly hoped with nothing but love;
Only dreamt o' a nest in a secluded cove-
Where the storms daren't damp our hope;
Where we'd learn to love more and cope.

But O! the bird has flown.
And I should have known...
Its wings stretched wasn't to warm the nest,
But to take flight to where it would find rest!

Lo, the nest- empty and cold.
Like Mother had always told,
As she would to a dream-lover son,
Of being true and wise ere it's gone.

But O! the bird has flown.
To find its peace, I reckon,
Having taught lessons of life with care,
From its heart and soul, it once laid bare.

If only I had known,
To make her my own!
If only I had shown,
The dreams I'd sown...

A speck in the horizon is what I see,
Of the bird and a dream never to be:
Determined wings across the skies brighter,
Dream taking wings to where dreams gather.

On the ground below, the nest is but all wet,
Soaked with' tears bidding farewell to sunset.
But come tomorrow the same Sun will rise
To warm the nest and teach me to be wise!

Yes, the bird has flown!
But no! I will not frown.
For the wind beneath its wings today,
Might carry her back to me someday!

To meet and depart that's been life's way;
To the wind of change, my dreams I'd lay:
If it could take away what I treasured most,
It'd bring me fairer wings for what I've lost.

When I'm Gone...

When I'm gone...
And there be none
To even remember me...
Lord, let me in Thy thoughts be.

When I'm gone...
And Mum's left alone,
Look into her loneliness;
Let her not suffer emptiness.

When I'm gone...
And my friends are won,
Help them chose their best,
That they may gladly find Thy rest.

When I'm gone...
Ere Kingdom come,
Let my dear brothers live
In love, that they may not grieve.

When I'm gone...
After my work's done,
Let my sisters live in honour,
And continue to find Thy favour.

When I'm gone...
Returned as Thy son,
Let me shelter in Thy place,
And rest eternal under Thy grace.

Woman of my Fantasy

Oh, the beauty of a woman in my fantasy!
Thought of her fills my spirit with ecstasy.
Moulded by the very hands of the Creator,
She's one of Heaven's privileged daughter.

Lithe, curvaceous body - so desirable;
Perfect figure to view from any angle;
Skin, so soft and silky smooth;
A touch puts minds to soothe.

Angelic face gushing with virgin-red blood;
Smile that'd melt thousand hearts to flood;
Bright-lit eyes to immerse, dissolve away;
Full amorous lips inviting your own to lay.

Flowing hair scented by Eden's flowers;
Washed in waters of crystal-clear rivers.
Hands that'd raise a soul with its wave,
Divinely shaped - to hold on ye'd crave.

Heart, no worldly sorrow would break.
Mind, no problem too grave to wreck.
Wisdom, enough to ignore and forgive,
And wit' love continue to grow and live.

Oh, the beauty of my fantasy woman!
To possess thee, desire o' a poor man.
To melt into thy bosom with the first kiss,
To merge forever as one in ecstatic bliss...

Yearning

Oh! To think of that day when she'd be mine,
And I, hers; to drink together of lover's wine.
There be none to prevent tight embraces,
Nor any power to spoil gentle caresses...

She'd have waited patiently for that moment;
Suppressed feelings like a gnawing torment;
Yearning to raise the seeds of love in her life;
Picturing her dual role as a mother and a wife.

Reward of the, sometimes, agonising wait,
Worth each day of solitude passed in faith-
Too sweet as patient Hope finds its pleasure
To create memory that'd remain as treasure.

Mortal Sojourn

Covering the miles of mortal sojourn,
Wit' dreams shattered and hope torn;
Doubting, can tomorrow be any better
Aft'r you'd stamped out the past bitter?

Warring against high principalities,
Your present is full of perplexities
Aggravated by abandoning friends
Who seem to prefer worldly trends.

You wonder if it's worth your effort
Of holding on to t'e unsecured fort,
And facing your nemesis head on;
Unsure if the battle's gonna be won.

Hark! oh soul, instead of givin' up
Tho' you drink from the bitter cup,
Nothin' lasts forever, not even 'joy'
In time, you'd find reason to enjoy.

Until such favourable day arrives,
Take care of how well life drives,
And continue to keep up the fight,
Instead of taking a cowardly flight.

Brave or coward, war's always on:
Some fight you've lost, some won;
Precious life's battle must continue,
Till death angel hoards its revenue.

So, live the days of your adventure,
Till that time HE halts your venture;
And no more shall you frown or cry
But smile as you declare, "I did try".

The Flag at Half-Mast

I stand all alone
In the land I belong,
Flying sad at half-mast,
Holding to my promise fast.

Waving in honour
At this darkest hour
Over my master's death-
Whose legacy reigns great.

My Father's gone!
His work's well done.
Humble writ is his story,
T'at ended wit' highest glory.

Ponder my colours;
Even Heaven favours
Ensign of truth and justice.
Pride of blood and sacrifice.

Wind of change,
Blows to rearrange
T'e order in places high,
T'at proudly I continue to fly!

I'm a living banner
The flag of my Father,
And of sons and daughters
Of t'e beloved Naga ancestors.

I shall keep flying free,
And make the nations see
The promise of God in a rainbow
To free the Nagas and end their sorrow.

Song of Love and Life

There's a song I carry
In my heart, as I tarry
In this world full of strife.
'tis a song o' love and life.

A love song heard by none;
Sung by my soul to the One
Who loves me above reason,
At all times, in every season.

A song of a life - full of gratitude
Sung with joy in humble attitude
To the God of the Second Chance
Who makes my soul leap & dance.

It's a song of a life that has grown
To love and live as one of His own,
Who betrayed self & God in the past,
But was allowed to rise from the dust.

Dust to dust, ashes to ashes - so it goes;
And to die someday, every mortal does,
But to suffer death ere the appointed day
That's the worst tragic role life could play.

So, to spare this heart from grief and pain
He revealed the reason why He was slain:
Love sent Him to the grave, but He arose,
And I'm redeemed to live out His purpose.

Thus, this song I carry in my heart,
That from His love I mayn't depart,
But keep singing and loving in mirth
To fulfil' His purpose behind my birth.

The Ignorant Fool

So, ye accept ye have lost it all;
Realizing too late to heed the call.
Ye'd stooped not but remained tall.
Knew not soon ye must indeed fall.

Ever seeking after fleeting pleasures,
Ye'd been missing ultimate treasures.
Often succumbing to peer pressure,
Letting precious life rot in vain leisure.

Soon shall the destined time come
For ye to journey alone back home;
And engulfed in an utter gloom,
Ye'd face the impending doom.

Ye knoweth that the end is near;
And for ye none bother nor care.
In life, ye mingled in the dark without fear.
In death, there be few to shed even a tear!

Sunday Morning Lines

Another morning, another new day.
No ordinary day, 'cause it's Sunday.
A day to be spent in humble adoration;
A day to be spent in self-introspection.

Trials and temptations no doubt I'd face,
But need I worry when I have His grace?
Then also, I've mercy and love so immense,
T'at with confidence, this day I'd commence.

How happy to be with the believers!
And be one of the blessed partakers,
In praises and prayers offered in faith.
And be all ears to w'at the Word sayeth.

Beware of the traps set up by the devil;
Hither and thither he prowls to do evil;
Seeking for the weak in spirit to devour,
T'at ye be called a child 'o God no more.

Beware thus, and idle not away.
But pray to know and keep His way.
And nourish thy spirit on this day,
To remain safe till another Sunday!

When Smiles Are Few

When things go cursed wrong,
And you feel you don't belong;

When friends are gone,
Leaving you dry, alone;

When smiles are few,
And courtesy is due;

When the present is filled with sorrow,
And there be less hope for tomorrow;

When the future itself seems lost,
And the past catches up like a ghost;

When tears fill life's cup,
and you feel like giving up...

Take heart, oh! precious soul.
For you are never too old
To set another beautiful goal,
That'd fetch the best gold!

Flow in faith with the timeless stream;
Will yourself to dream another dream,
And when you wake up you will see,
Life is not as bad as it seems to be!

The Lonely Lover

Alone, she feels lost and lonely.
The Sun, for her, has set too early.
Ere remembered by all so fondly,
Here, she misses company dearly.

The cold, icy wind of winter
Freezes her memories bitter,
Of that dark day last summer,
When death claimed her lover.

Times have passed, yet remains fear:
April showers remind of grief to bear.
In her deluded mind left utterly bare,
E'ery raindrop's mothered by her tear.

Autumn evokes in her mind of emptiness,
As she pines for his care and closeness.
Spring buds forth into solitariness,
As sorrows bloom into emptiness.

Her days pass in mournful tears;
Her nights filled with nightmares-
Of miseries which she alone bears.
Of future's ascribed toils and cares.

Lo! Death tolls no bell o' joy or gain.
But she'd learn to take flight again.
For dark death, nor sunshine or rain,
Shall claim the grace which remain!

The Gift of a New Dawn

How beautiful to be greeted by the new dawn,
When good God pulls the night's veil down;
Let the light infiltrate across the thin air,
While you fold up your morning gear.

My spirit rises to hear birds chirping.
My soul delights over brooks bubbling.
My heart rejoices o'er the gurgling streams.
My mind, ecstatic, fills up with hopeful dreams.

Lo, the steadfast faithful mountain!
The nature and life sustaining fountain,
The clouds looming in the azure sky above.
How the universe proclaims His glory and love!

Rest a while from your hectic chores and cares;
And behold His creations, their praise bears
Testimony of living out assigned roles
Preaching God to all ignorant souls.

Marvel not at the works of thy hands or wealth.
Look instead at the Hand caring thy health.
The same has created the vast universe;
To Him with words of praise converse.

A Blessed Day

When the cool breeze blows across your face
And awakens your senses to feel HIS grace,
As the beautiful morning humbly greets you,
That's the time you offer gratitude that's due
To the One who kept watch over you at night,
As you slept and dreamt till the morning light.

When the wind herds the looming clouds away
And the sunlight gently begins its toil of the day
Tenderly kissing and nudging awake the flowers,
And coaxing the petals to open for their lovers,
That's the right time for the lovers of the bloom
To start the day rejoicing over the night's gloom.

When the sunrays begin to dazzle-dance in mirth
With all creations on the surface of mother earth,
And the birds lend their song in melodious strain,
And the waters of brooks gurgle down the plains,
Take cue, my dear, and know it is a blessed day
For us to praise the Lord and live in our best way.

Christ's 'Circle of Friends'

Behold Him, just as any other mortal human,
Cameth He to His footstool as a Son of man.
Walketh, eateth and worketh like a common being,
Forsaking the heavenly abode where He had been.

He could have had a council of wise men,
Instead chooses him the lowly fisherman.
He could have been a friend of the emperor,
But preferred him the despised tax collector.

He could have earned the best of all the titles,
But more concerned was He for the gentiles.
He could have the hypocrites stone the prostitute,
Instead He allowed her into His heavenly institute.

Above all, He gave me a second chance to live,
Even though I had nothing of worth, to give.
Indeed, He brought me back from certain death,
Just because of His mercy and love so great.

I was but once, the worst of all known abusers
Of drugs and alcohol that killeth my honour.
But no more do I crave for the worldly trend,
For Jesus Christ, I found, is my only true friend.

Broken Vessel

An aimless spirit; a crying soul;
A dying body despised by all.
Life consumed by ill habits;
Living in pieces and bits
Of Hope fading away
Into that dark alley.
Like a vessel useless-
Lying in thousand pieces,
Broken and given up to decay
With what time and seasons pay
The sons and daughters who ignore
To pay heed to the call of the Father.
And yet, He has patiently waited
To make use what He created,
T'at His purpose be fulfilled,
As the created had willed
To make a turnaround.
So, from the dump ground
He picks up every single piece
Of the broken vessel in His grace,
Lovingly mends it with silver and gold.
Restores it- much better than one o' old
Begins to use it to glorify His Holy Name.

She Cares for Humanity

Perched on a balcony high,
She heaves a helpless sigh:
Her eyes fixed at the world;
Her mind on memories old.

She watches men and women;
The rich and the common men-
Ever busy in their own ways;
Ever ignorant o' the last days.

In pursuit of their ambitions,
Human race from all nations
Seemed to have fallen away;
Lost in 'evil games' they play.

Her eyes fill with sad tears
For all the people she cares.
She wipes not her teardrops,
But let 'em fall to raise hope.

She questions God's silence,
When men are losing sense,
Their body and soul, as well,
Unable to rise once they fell.

Men against men and nature
Spells doom for the future.
Past seemed much better,
But present is w'at matters.

Days are when she screams-
Wishing, it's just her dreams,
And she'd wake up to realize
Her hope with a new sunrise;

But each new day only offers
What God deems fit to proffer
This generation of much evil,
Lorded over and led by devil.

Perched on a balcony high,
She pleads God to be nigh,
And stop this Falling Away
Of His people gone astray.

She keeps praying in tears,
Hoping He'd incline His ears,
And fight for the human race
To save our soul in His grace.

He Sees and Does What's Best

O God, who can escape from Your eyes?
Who can ever hide himself with his lies?
All iniquities are laid bare in Your sight;
E'ery sinner's veil removed in Your light.

I was found as my soul sojourned to hell,
While my body lay grounded...where I fell.
Still, Your love picked me up from the filth,
And Grace and Mercy restored my health.

Though darker and rougher goes my way,
And all worldly cares press harder by day,
With patience in His tender love I can rest,
For my heart says, "He knows what's best."

On a Lonely Road

He walks a lonely road,
Wit' a heavy mental load,
To find a refuge of his own,
And make his purpose known.

He has chosen this path
To escape from evil wrath,
That had tormented his soul,
And made him bitterly cry foul.

He knows he's all alone,
And t'e path ruthlessly long;
He's been on it only for a while,
Carrying his hope past every mile.

He yearns for some rest,
But memories o' past wrest
And overwhelm his body frail,
To keep trudging this lonely trial.

Alone he must strive on,
Till the battle's finally won,
And he has sent all his critics
To revisit their own mental attics.

So, he walks a lonely road,
Hoping to unburden his load;
Wit' memory as his companion,
Wit' a dream and a will to carry on.

A Reason to Live, Love and Hope

When you feel the sky of your ambitions,
And the world of your hopes and dreams
Darken'd by some unexpected situations,
And faith seem to rush away like streams.

~

Do not forget there'll always be a rainbow,
Just like t'e lush green grass in a meadow,
As the sign of God's hope and a covenant,
T'at nothing in this world's e'er permanent.

~

You'd still be the butterfly that flutters by,
Or like eagles, that swiftly in the skies fly,
Or like the lovely rose that blooms away,
Or like a Dancing Quill that dances away...

~

For you have a pre-destined reason to live
Even more a wonderful reason to believe,
That the Lord created you for a purpose
To be "the butterfly for your Mama Rose."

~

And for all the other beautiful flowers as well.
So when the storm hits and things go unwell,
Take heart and remember that God is there
To help you soar above storms without fear.

Life - A Perilous Voyage

Life's often not what the eye sees.
A vessel sailing in the great seas-
Calm to a beholder on the shore;
Peril to hands that steer the oar.

Happy deck-hands on friendly water,
Settin' up proud sails on fair weather,
Soon may face the ravaging storm.
And none but the sea be safe from.

Take care thus, in your life's voyage.
Expect the unseen forces that ravage
Or steal the billowing wind out of your sails.
Be wise to reach destiny's home with hails!

Alive on Purpose

This life's not over though some may think so.
We still have miles to travel; many places to go.
The road stretches on past every unkind bend.
We have the will to carry on; a cause to defend.

Shattered dreams we'll revive.
Broken hearts can still survive.
And yes! We're alive to amend
What the world calls "The end."

We don't look down at the broken crayons-
They could still light life's empty pages on
By painting them in the colours of rainbow,
And reminding us of God's everlasting vow.

This life is not our own;
Soul has always known.
Broken but kept going,
It's the Master's doing.

We have chance to do best,
Till we finally come to rest.
So, mock not when you find us down.
We're also seeds that God had sown.

Wonder Why

Why would a man hoard wealth,
And by greed and power get lured,
At the cost o' his precious health,
Then spend his all to get cured?

Why would a man act and speak,
Like he has seen tomorrow's Sun,
And vex the path of 'em who seek
Their share of today's joy and fun?

Why would a man live and behave,
As if his life would last forever,
And to his vices remain a slave,
But to his fellow men a master?

Why would a man-evil and wicked,
Continue to survive and flourish,
While the righteous get picked
For the slightest wrong and perish?

Why would God prolong the life
Of a man, corrupt and dishonest,
Who, to his society, brings strife,
Corrupt even t'e ways of honest?

Unless the same God who made them,
And caused this little mind to wonder
Reveals the answer and act by His name,
Life would go on and I would still ponder...

Why, Oh, Why???

Death Be Not Proud

Oh cruel death, be not proud!
Nor wealth, our thought crowd.
Pray our health just be sound,
Whilst heart by God be found
By the Lord who heals wounds
Of our souls above our pounds.
Money comes and goes around;
Not life that's gone underground.

Why does wisdom keep hiding
While follies keep on prancing?
Why does a mortal suffer and die
Ere he finds answer to his 'why'?
The universe exhales answers;
So does the fragrance of flowers.
The whole of Creation calls out
To tell you what life is all about.
Care you to incline your ears
To the whispers of the stars?
Care you to hearken the Word
Uttered by the gracious Lord?
Halt, Oh dear, from thy busyness!
Respect and honour His holiness,
And you'd finally discover the reasons,
Why He's called a God o' all seasons.
Know ye not about your tomorrows?
It would herald unbearable sorrows.
Learn from the Lord about the future,
Even of the death of a mere creature.
Death be not proud, nor O ye, wealth!
For the Lord has gifted us with health
And with wisdom to accept the truth,
That ere we die we will bear His fruit.

Roses and Thorns

To reap the joy of blessings in days ahead
Let my heart be search'd thoroughly and led
By the spirit that has guided me to this age,
That I may keep on scripting each new page
With the tragi-comic stories which my life is.
May truth be told and glory and honour be His.

Let thorns find mention in the story of roses;
Let pain and relief be taken in balanced doses.
A rosy life sans worldly care is not believed,
Nor a life full, and ever happy could be lived.
Light is best appreciated because of the dark;
So are good records in presence of ill remark.

Yet to suffer such agony men has not known,
Life would complain for being wearied down
With the burden load upon the tired shoulder,
And a mental burden that shan't be a wonder.
Alas! the pathetic life of mortals who toil away,
As those of less intellect make merry and gay.

Let me remember through this pain I suffer,
That life's not all about joy; but what it offers.
Let me today, experience the fires of sorrow,
That I mayb e well-prepared for the morrow.
And if I could work to lessen the pain in future,
So be it! According to His purpose as I mature.

Taking Thoughts to the Sea

Oft' when emotion sweeps over me,
I'd take my thoughts to the vast sea.
Sailing away to a secluded destination.
Where sorrow, nor grief has recreation.

To the void of nothingness,
I'd exhale all my bitterness;
Let the waves wash away my loneliness,
And release my feelings into emptiness.

Alas! If only the sea would remain calm!
To my sorrows, act as comforting balm.
If only it would be sans the raging storm.
And embrace my grief in its eternal form.

Painful thought is but, an illusion.
To many, their source of confusion.
Still, to escape from its cruel torment,
I'd hazard the sea for my sad moment.

My Lighthouse

There is a Lighthouse in the Emerald Isle.
It lights my path as I walk mile after mile
Towards my destination Heaven prepared.
My journey may be hard but I'm not scared
For the Light is there to guide and lead me
Through every "twist and turn" I mayn't see.

Once a sojourner in the island of vanities
Tryin' to escape from life's harsh realities,
Now, I tread the narrow path under grace
Of my God who will let me finish my race.
For what He has started He will complete
Using Heaven's powers that never deplete.

And so the Lighthouse in a land distant:
To help remind me of His love constant,
And of His purpose behind my creation,
That I may love and script with passion,
And not give up for hurt, pain, or sorrow,
But keep living with HOPE for tomorrow.

The Portrait of a Dancing Soul

The Child within her soul cried to be freed
To pursue her love and perform kind deed.
'twas not asking much from heaven's view,
Nor was it a demand worded weirdly new.

Many times she had put her desires to rest-
Desires of a child who wish'd to be the best
In all interests and voyages she might set sail-
Desires to be realised- when none could tell.

Until one glorious dawn she let go and let God.
But she cautioned self never to spare the rod.
And the child took off to live out her passion,
And clear her Mama's doubts and confusion.

She dipped her brush in the well of heaven
And painted her canvas t'at was God-given.
And when she was satisfied with her Work,
She left it in Mama's room w'en 'twas dark.

As the morning rays filtered across the room
To dispense any shadows of the dark gloom,
Mama stirred and hearkened to the call 'arise'
And awoke to be greeted wit' a huge surprise.

T'ere on her table stood an awesome painting.
It mirrored her colourful soul t'at was dancing.
It was the dance of a freed soul, of her dream,
Dancing and melting away in Heaven's stream.

Oh, how for a thousand times she has seen
Her soul being carried away into the ocean,
Where she'd dance away with the lover King
In great ecstasy and joy such has ne'er been!

She kissed the surreal Work of Art in tears;
And no matter w'at be all her worldly cares,
Promised to entertain the Child within her
By dancing her heart out as she deem fair.

The God of all Seasons

There are times when I wonder,
When certain situation runs joy asunder,
And replace it with perplexities
To fill this hopeful life with uncertainties.

Seasons of goodness and gaiety
Robbed suddenly by a feeling of anxiety
Over circumstances that come
To snatch away joy from hearts and home.

Hearts grow weary; mind taxed.
Confusion creeps in and turns life laxed.
Problems sight'd all around you
Becomes the centre of life and dreams too.

Finding no rescue you weep, cry...
Your soul searches God and asks 'but why?'
Still you find no answer, no hope.
Dark spell continues and alone you cope.

Frustrated... still you keep praying,
Hoping to keep holding on and keep trying;
Wishin' to ne'er let go of life dear
After having tasted joy and overcome fear.

When a fading hope least expects,
A small, still voice to your heart directs;
And you know it's God responding
To your problems and answers pending.

The small, still voice clearly says,
"Thou made problems rule over thy days,
And thine season became worse.
I wasn't made the centre of thy universe."

"Where was I when ye verily tried
To solve thy problems thyself and failed?
Did ye allow I, the Lord, thy space
That I could cover them with my grace?"

It dawns where you've gone wrong:
Your ignorant self-had tried to be strong
'stead of letting God do your battle,
And allow the ravaging storms to settle.

You say "Lord God, forgive please"
Gives Him space; your problems cease
To vex and torment life any further.
For He makes our dark seasons better.

Masterpieces of Love

High up in the paradisiacal hub of the Creator
Is a gallery, massive and filled with splendour.
It houses the painting works of the good Lord
Of e'ery human created accordin' to His Word.

Each painting depicts God's beautiful purpose
For an individual, before age and time dispose
His mortal body back to where he came from,
And his freed soul in heaven or fiery hell roam.

High up in the paradisiacal hub of the Creator
Is anoth'r gallery - smaller but wit' glory greater.
Displayed on its walls are paintings of people
Who have lived righteously and in ways simple.

Those who lived in opposition to God's plan-
Be they as single or family or tribe or as clan,
Find no place or mention in the other gallery.
For against God they sowed seeds of rivalry.

Saddened to the core our God awaits patiently
For those who're led astray to return repentantly.
He longs for them to understand about His love,
With which He paints masterpieces from above.

Hear ye ignorant soul! Your life is a masterpiece,
God Himself painted that His plan may not cease,
But succeed and find place in His treasure trove,
As a reminder that we're masterpieces o' His love.

In Search of God

Alone she cries aloud,
Looking up at the clouds,
Wondering if God would be
In the fluffy mass for her to see;
But He's not to be seen in the clouds.

She searches the deep,
Where He is said to keep
The mystery of seas hidden
Amongst the creatures unseen;
But HE's not to be seen in the deep.

In the high mountains
And crystal-clear fountains;
Over the hills and plain valleys;
In the busy streets and dark alleys-
She searches but He ain't to be found.

She goes to the church
And continues her search,
But her search proves futile.
She stops and rests for a while,
Then hears a still, small voice speak.

"Did you search your heart?
I've been dealing with your hurt,
That caused you to search for Me.
O, if only you had known where I'd be,
You would've searched only your heart."

The Flower of Grace

There's a wonderful story told
About a flower that never grows old,
Nor withers away with season
But keeps blooming for godly reason.

It's the Heaven's Flower of grace
That unfolds its petals for human race;
And spreads the fragrance of love
To men and nature as in paradise above.

Beneath the shade of its petals,
Rests dreams and ambitions of mortals,
Nurtured by their toils and cares;
Brought into a reality by those who dare.

Naked eyes may not have seen,
But the flower of grace has always been
Blooming fair in the vast expanse,
Like a colossal beauty in eternal trance.

It blooms under the eternal Light,
Reflecting the nature of the Lord bright
Upon everything, seen or unseen;
Filling the universe with God's love even.

How blest to wear the fragrance,
Spread it around with this gifted chance,
And see love bloom in the heart
Of e'ery man before Time calls to depart.

The story of the Flower of grace
Is woven with love from the sacred place;
And is shared as per w'at He saith:
That by grace are we saved, through faith.

The Accomplished Soul

In a realm of glory, she stands,
Holding the universe in her hands;
It's the universe of her life and family-
The universe she helped create tenderly
With her love and kind words and deeds.
She has worked to remove the weeds
That had grown to suppress mind
And caused life to lack behind.

It is her own universe of Light
Where hope shines eternal bright;
And the first seed of love sown by her
Has grown well to bring hearts together,
To reap a bountiful harvest for the Lord;
That souls may praise in one accord
The God who sent her in His grace
To make her world a better place.

Hers is story others would tell
To kids who'll remember her well,
As a loving soul who played her part
In effecting change in hardened hearts.
She lost no souls that Heaven gave her,
But guided all back to Him with care,
As her love for each paved the way
To take her to the Realm far away.

Dancing in the Storm

Watch the trees gently sway,
As they happily dance away
In and with the blowing wind
To delight our eyes and mind.

Listen to what the leaves say
Of living life in a splendid way;
Caring least about the past,
Dancing as if it was the last...

Hear their laughter in the storm
As they revel in their best form.
They bother not for the morrow,
Nor worry about how they grow.

In dying they turn into ground
For life to spring forth around,
That the cycle would carry on,
And living be not only for own.

Behold the trees, dancing sans care:
They have no time to stand or stare.
Stripped naked they still stand tall;
Unconcerned when they would fall.

Would men care to learn from them,
And dance in the storm sans shame;
Standing tall even in the dark season;
Believing there'd be a divine reason?

God at Work

(Creating Masterpieces)

So, you missed the Light show yesterday?
Don't you worry for today is another day.
Watch God paint the sky in His own way
Wit' colours that'd take your breath away.

He dips His brush in the well of rainbow,
Like a wand that effects a magical glow
In every colour He brings up in pleasure
To paint and splash around in His leisure.

What our eyes see at any given moment
Enthrals us and leaves the heart content;
For He delights in pleasing His creations
Wit' ethereal Art t'at portrays His passion.

Ever at work He does the same wit' men;
Working on lives in the best way He can;
Creating masterpieces from empty lives,
T'at through His work joy we may derive.

Yet how often we've remained ignorant
Of His beauty and purpose so important!
All because of our worldly cares and toils,
Caring not if we're growing well in His soil.

Awake, arise and behold His light show!
Learn from the colours of the Rainbow-
Promise of love God leaves as His Mark;
They remain the same; so does the Arc.

Dreams and Hopes

Dreams I carry,
As I tarry
In this mortal frame,
Not for fame,
But in His Name
To lift the shame,
That sin has placed
Upon souls disgraced
For their dark habits,
As they lie in pits
Dug by their vices
Out of wrong choices.

Dreams I carry,
With hope I marry,
And take it to the Altar
Of the Creator;
That He may bless
And help me harness
The desires of my heart,
As I make a fresh start,
In all humility,
With this opportunity
To sow Love-seed
In the life of those in need.

I may grow weary,
But He'll help carry
My hopes and dreams.
When my enemy screams
"Impossible" at my face,
I will turn to His grace
And continue to strive on
Till the final battle is won.
Dark experiences of past
Shall stir up The Dust
And allow them to shine
In the Light Divine.

Living Best Despite...

As hard as it seems,

The purpose of life

And all our dreams,

Despite ills or strife,

Is to stand in any place

With our head held high,

In the strength of grace,

Under His watchful Eye.

Behold a solitary wildflower,

Caring least where it grows:

It bothers not for its grower,

But to bloom pretty it knows.

It blossoms its best for all,

And dances with the wind-

Pleasing our sense and soul;

Acting as balm to the mind.

Living for the moment,

It doesn't count the days,

Or ever stays dormant;

It romances wit' sun rays.

Here today, gone tomorrow!

Why live or die with sorrow

When we'd all give our best

And bloom pretty till we rest?

The Journey of Life

Life is but a journey, man a sojourner.
T'e road you take decides your future.
Multitudes chose t'e easy, broad road
And sojourn with their iniquities' load.
Unsure of what lies over t'e next bend;
Fearful t'e journey might abruptly end

T'ose treadin' t'e road strait and narrow
Worry not about t'e past or t'e morrow
Carry an ensign of t'e Cross with pride,
Miles after miles, walking side by side.
Each step taken with prayers and faith.
Each day a lit'l closer to Heaven's gate.

Some others return from t'e easy road
Leaving behind their sin's burden load
And hasten to tread on t'e narrow road.
Being cleansed by the Saviour's blood
And given a chance for new beginning,
And t'e hope of joy that's never ending.

Mirrors and Reflections

There is a mirror for every human being,
That reflects the state of a soul unseen.
It uncovers lies and hidden acts of men,
And reveals the truth that'll ever remain.

The mirror discloses every dark secret;
And causes the heart to feel and regret
For all the wrongs that can't be undone;
For all the precious years, forever gone.

Little words and deeds of kindness
Reflect the nature of His goodness,
Casting upon the image of the doer,
And making the face shine brighter.

Little acts of love from a pure heart
Reflect a picture formed outta mirth
Of a soul ready to share with others,
What's given by the heavenly Father.

All that eyes see as our reflections
Are but the pictures of our actions.
Every good seed bears good image;
Every bad seed rot before its age.

He who, to the truth turns and pay heed,
And in the hearts o' brethren sow seed
Of love in simulation of the greater love,
Reaps just rewards from Heaven above.

He presents an image perfected in time:
Image that bears mark of his age prime,
While he chooses to follow what is right
And stays within the reach of God's light.

Will Heaven Miss Us?

Will heaven miss us, my dear?
When life's journey ends here,
And all our cares laid to rest;
And all our deeds put to test.

Will heaven miss us, my dear?
When truth makes itself clear
To reveal the life, we had known;
To reveal the lies we had sown.

Will heaven miss us, my dear?
When judgement sounds fair
For all the things we had done;
For all the chances that's gone.

Will heaven miss us, my dear?
When God claims all His share
Of honour He alone deserves;
Of glory His Thorne preserves.

Will the place He has prepared
In His love and grace, be barred
For our entrance for all eternity?
For the life we'd lived in vanity?

Hearken to the Voice that says
"Prepare ye, for dark, grim days
When ye shall run for life in vain,
And Earth shall groan with pain."

"Prepare ye, thy heart in His soil.
Make honest count of every toil,
Make blessed of what's God-given
Tat ye may find a place in heaven."

The Gentle Whisper

Soft and tender is His Voice,
That makes my heart rejoice.
It brings me hope and peace,
And let my heartaches cease.

It comes as a gentle whisper
To rescue my soul in despair.
It brings to life my numb sense
In my hour of complete silence.

For many seasons, I have lived
As a fool who had not believed
In the saving grace of our Lord,
Or in the promises of His Word.

And yet He kept watch over me;
Opened my eyes and let me see
All beautiful things I never knew,
Tat the old may usher in the new.

As the wind blows in from the west,
It brings message of Love and Rest
To calm my mind & soothe my heart,
Tat I may be freed from all past hurt.

How wonderful to hear His whisper!
Of Hope and Love beyond compare,
Carried on wings of Mercy and Grace,
To wrap my soul in its warm embrace.

Being the Change

She walks down the street,
Smiling despite the summer heat,
Oozing love and confidence;
Her face worthy of remembrance.

She is clothed in humility,
And her heart beats for humanity.
Her smile is contagious;
Her beauty a boon to eyes curious.

It wasn't so a summer ago,
Until she realised it better to let go
Of all the abuses and hurt,
That the world sowed in her heart.

She chose to be the change,
And in her own little ways rearrange
The things within her reach
To effect change & let action preach.

Generous smile she lends
To strangers as she would to friends,
Whose joy and happiness
Have been shadowed by selfishness.

The change first began in her,
And from her to family, far and near,
Then spread on to neighbours
Who in turn influenced many others.

The seed of change has today,
Grown to erase the ills of yesterday
From the mind of colony people,
Who have turned to live life humble.

Realizing the power of change,
She's prepared to smile at any challenge,
That may come along her way,
As she walks down the street every day.

Her message to the multitude,
Through her smile and friendly attitude,
Is accepted by all in gratitude
To what she offers mankind as a tribute.

Dance with Me

Come to Me,
And dance with Me.
Rise up, cross the Line;
Merge your heart wit' Mine.

Don't be afraid,
For Love has said;
I will lead you my dear.
With Me you needn't fear.

Leave your past;
Arise from the dust;
Just give Me your hand;
We'll dance in the hall grand.

Leave your cares;
Bury your nightmares.
I know your heart my child.
Do not remain in a desert wild.

Don't you know...
Host of angels bow
To receive a willing heart,
That dances with Me in mirth?

Don't you know...
I love the dance flow
From your soul into Mine,
As I tune up the rhythm fine?

Just take a step,
And I will gladly clap,
And take you in My arms,
While Heaven rolls its Drum.

Just take a step;
Move a leg and tap
To the beats of My heart,
And I'll lead you from the start.

Rescued Hope

She puts on a smile,
As she walks another mile
With a heavy burden
In a path few have trodden.

She tries to act tough
Even when time goes rough,
And her mind overcast
With memories of sad past.

She tries to act brave,
And strives harder to save
What is left of her life,
As a mother and as a wife.

Yet when the day's over
And night spreads its cover,
Her heart weeps unheard
O'er the abuse she'd suffered.

In creeps the darkness
To her crying soul's distress,
And robs her of sleep,
As she prays her soul to keep.

Up in the heavenly realm,
Where God delights in her dream,
Angels leave their abode
To comfort & lift her burden load.

Soon she would realise
The Hand of God, and be wise
To understand His grace,
That works to brighten her face.

All her fears would flee;
She'd grow again & bloom free
In the Garden of Love;
Watched & tended by God above.

She'd learn to love again;
Hope and strength, she'd regain;
No longer would she strain
To put on a smile or laugh again.

Finding Love to Live Again

She stirs in her bed and lets out a yawn,
As the sun rises to usher in a new dawn.
The air rings with morning birds' melody,
That sends thrill through her rested body.

She opens the windows and smiles away;
Grateful for the gift of another lovely day.
The gentle wind caresses her lithe figure
To arouse sense of delight and love pure.

Sweet fragrance of flowers reminds her
Of the pleasant scent worn by her lover,
Whose mortal life ended one cold winter
Leaving only a story writ upon the water.

Left alone, with tears as her companion,
She oft' wondered why life should go on,
Till she met Love; and Love rescued her
From brokenness to life's sunny chapter.

Love opened her eyes to revel in nature;
Gave her solace and hope for the future.
Love taught her to overcome loneliness
And allowed her to discover happiness.

Her senses - benumbed at her lover's loss
Come alive, today, to feel the nature close.
So, the fragrance of flowers of every kind,
The melody of birdsong, the gentle wind...

When clouds of doubt loom over her head,
She'll rest assured knowing God ain't dead.
Believing in the soft tender voice that says
"Peace, be still; soon there'd be better days."

Love

Love, how beautiful spells your name!
You cover up my flaws and shame,
And fills my heart with a passion
To pen about you unto nations,
T'at mortals from every race
May learn of your embrace,
That sustains the World
And makes men bold.

In you there's no fear;
For you hold me so dear.
You turn my sorrow into joy;
And give me reasons to enjoy
Life's best moments with Hope.
You teach me how to wisely cope
With every situation t'at I would face,
That I may finish my race in His grace.

You blessed me with a Story
To tell about Thee and of His glory.
You gave me the hope to live
And taught me to trust and believe.
For my sins you paid the cost;
But for you, I would have been lost.

Tears and Hope

When the world goes silent,
And the Sun seems content
Hiding behind the dark clouds,
Her soul wishes to protest aloud;
And ask why she's still kept alive,
W'en from life she can't derive
Peace that had once been
With her, though unseen.

Of her tears that flows,
Like a river, as life grows,
Into the sea of utter despair,
She wishes it's all a nightmare.
But she knows it to be a reality
Born out of a mortal's vanity
Of living life wit'out belief,
Or hope of any relief.

She has lost her lover.
Her soulmate and a giver
Of hope, strength and grace,
Her source of love to embrace.
Emotions have turned stronger,
But only dreams o' him linger.
Luscious lips have dried,
Heart has only cried.

Her spirit remains low;
Tear-soaked is her pillow.
Her head rests, not her mind,
That plays memory left behind.
Sleep eludes her wearied body.
She wishes for somebody
Who'd her sorrow keep,
And lull her to sleep.

Unasked, God steps
Into her life and wraps
Her sorrows in His grace;
And grief He leaves no trace.
He hastens the clouds away
And gifts her a sunny day,
That w'en it's tomorrow
She'll no more sorrow.

Soon she will realise,
Grow and become wise.
She will learn to accept life,
Deal with fate and any strife.
As days, like clouds pass by,
She'd stop asking just why,
But will hers'lf to fight on
Till life's battle is won.

The Solitary Painter

Behold Him, single in the Eastern Bed
Yon solitary Heavenly Head!
Painting and musing by Himself;
Witness the show for your good self
Alone He painstakingly paints
For mortals, angels and saints.
Wow! Witness the master strokes,
As the first rays paints even the rocks.

No genius painter ever did such an art
For nature and races living poles apart,
Using colours from the rainbows;
Even mother nature solemnly bows.
For an art so splendid was ne'er seen
From the past till present hasn't been.
The Artist only wishes to remind
About His love to men of every kind.

The morning sky does display
His presence every time, each day
Of the beauty so rare and rich,
That we may watch, learn and teach
The ignorant to appreciate and honour,
And be blessed to find His favour.
Breaking the shackles of inequality,
And together, live as one in unity.

The captivating Art ne'er was heard,
But soon would have been shared
By the elect to make understand,
That His Glory we can't withstand.
And thus, His Hand and His brush,
For humanity to witness and not rush.
Lest they trample their own relations
And invite chaos and confusions.

Will no one tell me what He paints?
Ere this soul gets confused and faints.
Perhaps, memories of the perfect Art
For old, unhappy, and miserable start.
And battles long ago well-fought
Still remains in His good thought.
Or is it for some more humble lay,
Familiar matter of yesterday?

Whatever the theme, He paints;
Ne'er can be compared with saints,
For His Art could have no ending;
Even as He works in Fields singing.
I watched, motionless and still;
And, as I mounted up the hill,
The image in my mind I bore,
Long after it was seen no more.

My Life
(In Lines and Rhymes)

Standing tall,
Loved by all;
Deceived by the devil
To inculcate habits evil.

Despised by all,
Following the Fall;
Confused and rejected
For drugs he injected.

Abusing his own body,
Till he turned into nobody;
Treading the path to hell,
Leaving a sad tale to tell.

The Lord Himself intervened,
By grace, had him convinced
The worth of his soul;
Paid heed to His call.

Rescued from a certain death,
Gave a chance to live till date;
Dawns Realisation
Makes confession.

Repented for all despicable sins
Through prayers & songs he sings;
Introduced to God of new beginnings
After wasted period of futile longings.

Discovers God's unconditional love,
As angels sing in the Heaven above.
A new venture starts,
Being healed in all parts

Begins a new venture
For the betterment of future;
Starts to scribble away
His past story, day by day.

He understands the worth of his Quill,
Keeps dancing according to His Will.
Thus, he says, "HERE I AM!"
For he knows now he's not the same!

Gifted the Keys, Light and the Staff
He desires to & have the last laugh
That those who comes to the school
Would never be considered a fool.

Tangoing with God

She's growing old but still dances mild;
For within her heart is a beautiful child,
Reflecting essence of purity & innocence,
While spreading pretty flowers' fragrance.

Yes, old is her but she is still a child;
Born wit' a purpose in the world wild
To represent unwavering faith & love,
As deemed fit by the Heaven's above.

Therefore, she tangoes with the Lord,
Learnt the moves by reading the Word
On the water's in the Ocean of Love;
Dancing & resting finally in His Cove.

Old but with a pure heart of a child,
She's never wavered or grown wild.
For she's been living wit' faith steadfast
And has vowed to dance on till the Last.

Old and yet a child for the Lord,
She has kept intact belief's Cord,
And so she dances with love and grace;
One chosen by God from the entire race.

Swift steps and moves so graceful-
An epitome of all children beautiful.
Fearless & unmindful of the dance floor,
For she entered through Heaven's door.

Oh, how the good Lord loves to dance
Wit' her- old but gifted wit' best chance
To keep tangoing happily & tirelessly,
Moving in perfect rhythm & fearlessly.

Old but wit' the child's heart and mind,
She's but one of the most unique kind,
Whom the Lord has chosen to tango wit',
That her Love may always remain sweet.

This Too Shall Pass

Abandoned - all alone in doubt.
Foresee the battles to be fought.
Struggling hands reaching out-
Discovering there is none about.

Groping in the darkness;
Finding yourself helpless.
Have I been so reckless,
To shed tears ceaseless.

Lonely, tho' friends be many.
Left to be in tears' company;
Left to suffer such a tragedy,
Left to soak up such misery.

Signs, I could have divined!
I could've used my right mind.
Alas! Time, I cannot rewind;
And life, I can't lose or bind.

So, the death; so, the tears.
Untimely, for all his fears.
Our cry he no longer hears-
Freed from all mortal cares.

You're gone, not your memory.
We shall pass on your legacy
To our offspring, for posterity
Till we're together for eternity.

Lo! This is our darkest season,
And there'd always be a reason
But the same won't go on & on.
This too shall pass and be gone.

Scars of my Battles and Wars

Of my personal battles and wars
I carry many big and small scars.
In the eyes of the world it is ugly,
But I've learnt to take it as lovely.
For I lived to tell about each scar
Even to those peoples from afar.

Each ugly scar bears a testimony
Of life overcast by clouds gloomy.
Mortals will one day see and learn,
That they need to battle and earn
Their own scars to keep living on
Wit' stories and lessons they own.

What men laugh at and call ugly now
No more will be called so tomorrow.
For when they understand from IT
They'd have come out from the pit,
And survived to tell their own story
To give our Lord all honour and glory.

To Strive... Till Death

To run from darkness to light;
To keep fighting the good fight;
To go walking till the last mile,
And wear your crown with smile.

To keep running the good race;
To live life worthy of His grace;
To keep chasing your dreams'
And find joy flow like streams.

To keep faith constant;
And from evil distant;
To never give up but try,
Till your blood turn dry.

For heavens so decreed,
That man of every creed,
Strive till his last breath,
To have his reward great.

One-way, Second Chance Ride

My life is a one-way, second chance ride.
My destiny is what He makes me decide
Wit' the freewill to choose wrong or right,
And be of the dark world or wit' the Light.

I turn regrets into lessons I should learn.
The past is gone; I cannot make a U-turn
And go back to reclaim all my lost years,
When I became the reason o' much tears.

My ride's slow & bumpy; the road narrow;
I know not what waits for me tomorrow;
Wind of adversity blows against my face,
That shan't deter me to keep up my pace.

Milestones of memories I leave behind.
Of the bitter past I choose not to rewind;
For w'at was done then, can't be undone.
W'at matters is now & it too will be gone!

Of the sharp bends of ugly circumstance,
T'at put my progress into a state o' trance,
I know I can count on His help and grace,
And He alone shall let me finish this race!

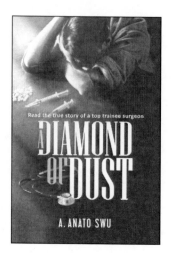

Loved 'The Dancing Quill'? Then order 'A Diamond of Dust' that tells of his life story of how a devoted son to his parents, entered a prestige medical school to train as a top surgeon. But later he would need help himself when... a one-time drug experience took him on a journey of an addict for 20 years.

'Diamonds of Dust' records, through experience, lucid accounts of not only what drugs and alcohol does to a person, but how to prevent you and your own children from becoming another statistic as its victim.

This book will encourage and give hope to families who have been affected by drugs and suicide.

To purchase visit
www.MauriceWylieMedia.com

INVITE THE AUTHOR

Anato now travels the world sharing his poetry and giving advice, lectures to government bodies, schools, churches and groups on how to deal with, and spot addiction.

If you would like to invite him to speak at your group, feel free to contact him at author@MauriceWylieMedia.com

MAURICE WYLIE MEDIA
Inspirational Christian Publisher
Based in Northern Ireland and distributing across the world.

www.MauriceWylieMedia.com